HTML & CSS FOR BEGINNERS

Your Step by Step Guide to Learn Easily
HTML & CSS Programming in 7 Days

iCode Academy

HTML & CSS FOR BEGINNERS
Copyright © 2017 by iCode Academy.
All rights reserved.

TABLE OF CONTENTS

INTRODUCTION

HTML is an acronym for Hyper Text Mark-Up Language. It is the main programming language used to develop websites. It acts as a framework of sorts where different elements like color, video, images, flash animation, etc. could be added later on.

This book will help you understand HTML's syntax and semantics, which will allow you to create a website completely from scratch. We'll teach you how to lay down the foundations—the backbone—of a website and then add aesthetic elements later on using Cascading Style Sheets or what's commonly known as CSS.

Back in the day, website creation and development would only go as far as one's imagination. Website developers of yesteryears had to get specialized education just to be able to learn a programming language and start developing websites, applications, etc. This was an extremely grueling process and would often times become the deterring factor for students. However, when HTML was introduced, website creation and develop got a whole lot easier.

Because of HTML's simplistic syntax and semantics, it significantly reduced a website's creation time by a considerable amount of time. In addition, most developers of today make use of HTML editors that have features like predictive input, which lessens coding and debugging time significantly. Helpful as these HTML editors may be, keep in mind that these programs are not foolproof and their effective still solely depends on the person wielding them.

This why knowing and fully understanding HTML is still crucial in being an effective and efficient website builder.

HTML editors usually offer an auto-correct feature which saves you the trouble of looking through long lines of code just to find the syntax error. However, there may be times when it'll perceive something as an error even though its actually not. This is what most programmers call a "false-positive". To prevent any false-positive changes made by an HTML editor, you may have to implement your desired changes manually. Doing this will obviously require an intermediate level of understanding of HTML.

If you're planning to create, develop and host your own website. Prudence requires you, the website owner, to at least have an intermediate level of understanding of HTML. Having a firm grasp of HTML's syntax and semantics allows you to effectively translate your vision of how you want your website to look like into code. Also, as a website owner who understands HTML, you have two advantages. The first advantage is that you won't be restricted to just whatever an HTML editor dishes out. Second, since you understand HTML yourself, you won't have to call and hire a web developer just to apply some minor changes into your website.

With that in mind, let's go ahead and start your HTML journey.

CHAPTER 1:
HTML FUNDAMENTALS

HTML describes itself as a mark-up language. In fact, it is an acronym for Hyper Text Mark-up Language. What does it mark-up and what does it use to mark-up elements? In HTML, marking up website elements such as video, images, and text-based content are done with the use of tags.

Tags are basically markers that distinguish particular content from others within an HTML file. Marking content with tags usually involve enclosing the content within an opening tag and a closing tag. HTML makes use of a variety of tags to distinguish different kinds of content in a website; all of which we will be discussing in detail in the preceding chapters of this book.

Back in the day, about 90% of a website's core is written in HTML. Aesthetic elements such as colors, shapes, forms, etc. were also handled by HTML. Everything was put in one basket, so to speak. This made debugging tedious and confusing, since the number of tags and attributes that a programmer must look into are overwhelming. This led the powers that be to create an HTML sub-component that would solely deal with the aesthetics of a website, while HTML exclusively handled the laying of a website's framework. This is how CSS or Cascading Style Sheet came to be.

Think of HTML as a website's skeleton and muscles, while CSS is a website's skin. CSS per se is a sub-component of HTML. However, CSS may also be regarded as a separate entity. It is separate in a sense that it has its own syntax and its core code is not entirely included in the main HTML document.

Incorporation of CSS in an HTML document is done through the use of CSS descriptors. How to use HTML and CSS together will also be discussed in the later chapters of this book. So, without further ado, let's get started in making an HTML document.

To start making a basic HTML file or document, you must first create a file type declaration tag at the top. Look at our basic HTML document below:

```
1    <!DOCTYPE html>
2    <html>This is how to start an HTML document!
3    </html>
```

Before we proceed, keep in mind that the number that precedes each line of our HTML code are put in place to serve only as a guide when pertaining to a specific line of code. It is not included in the actual HTML code.

Moving forward and looking at our HTML code above, we started our HTML file with the <!DOCTYPE html> tag in line one. This tag's sole purpose is to tell the browser that the programming language that it's about to read is HTML.

Mozilla Firefox, Google Chrome, Microsoft Edge, Microsoft Internet Explorer, and Opera are just a few examples of browsers that can interpret HTML code. The <!DOCTYPE html> tag is what's called as an all-encompassing tag. It doesn't require any closing tags since it encompasses the entirety of the HTML document regardless of its size.

In line two of our code, we started the main body of our HTML file with the <html> tag. As what was previously mentioned, tags usually involve enclosing website elements within an opening and closing tag. In our HTML code's case, We've enclosed a simple text-based content between an opening <html> tag and a closing </html> tag.

7

Every element of your website, be it paragraphs, images, videos, or audio, should be placed between the opening <html> tag and the closing </html> tag. This makes sure that they will be interpreted by the browser as HTML. The browser Any code that falls outside the <html> and </html> tags will not be interpreted by a browser as HTML and would most likely produce an error in your HTML code.

Of course, after we've placed every element within the <html> tag and the </html> tag, we need to distinguish those elements from each other. We do this by giving those elements a tag of their own. The type of tag each element would get would depend on what type of content they are in the first place. If you have a paragraph content, then it would be enclosed between an opening <p> tag and a closing </p> tag. If you have a primary heading content, then it would be enclosed between an opening <h1> tag and a closing </h1> tag, and so forth.

This process of putting tags within tags is called "Nesting". Nesting is done all throughout HTML. Let's look at the code below for an example of nesting:

```
1       <first tag>
2               < second tag>
3                       <third tag>Learning how to Nest in
HTML</third tag>
4               </second tag>
5       </first tag>
```

Looking at the example above, we opened our first tag in line one, followed by a second tag in line two and followed by the third tag in line three. The first thing you'll notice when nesting tags is that as we put tags within tags, the level of indentation increases. Indentation doesn't have any real impact on code, aside from the fact that it makes reading HTML code easy and non-confusing.

Indentation also helps the programmers reading the code to distinguish the parent tag from the children tag. Looking at our nesting code again, we can see that the first tag is the parent tag of the second tag (the second tag being contained within the first tag). The second tag in this case acts as the parent tag for the third tag and the children tag of the first tag. Lastly, the third tag is just a children tag of the second tag since there's no fourth tag that would make it a parent of.

As you may have already guessed after going through our nesting code example, closing nested tags should start from the most recently opened tag and then working your way backwards. Also, closing parents tags should have the same level of indentation as their opening tag counterparts. As you can see in our previous code, the closing second tag has the same level of indentation as its opening tag. The same can be said with the closing first tag. If a children tag is not a parent of any other tag, then its closing tag can be placed on the same line as its opening tag. This is clearly evident with the third tag in our previous example.

HTML Head
Now that we have some of the nitty-gritty out of the way, let's discuss the first key element when starting to create your website with HTML; the HTML Head.

An HTML file is basically divided into two parts: the body and the head. The HTML head is where the general information of your website/HTML document is contained. Take a look at the HTML code below which has the head element:

```
1    <!DOCTYPE html>
2    <html>
3            <head>
4                    <title>My very first Website</title>
5            </head>
6    </html>
```

As you can see in our code above, the HTML head is distinguished by the <head> and </head> tags. General information about y our website would be nested inside these head tags, and as you can clearly see in line four of our code, there's a title element called "My very first Website" nested inside the head tag.

Again, want can't stress the importance of closing tags enough. Most programmers, even expert ones, sometimes forget to close tags properly. This often leads to backtracking lines of code just to find that one line with an unclosed tag. Backtracking lines of code to rectify an unclosed tag is okay as long as you're dealing with less than a hundred lines of HTML code. However, backtracking thousands of lines of code can be very grueling.

HTML Body
After discussing the HTML head, let's now move on to the HTML body. The HTML body is where the main content of the website is contained. Let's look at an example of an HTML body below:

```
1       <!DOCTYPE html>
2       <html>
3               <head>
4                       <title>My very first Website</title>
5               </head>
6               <body>
7                       <p>This is my very first website. </p>
8               </body>
9       </html>
```

Remember when we said that an HTML file is divided into two parts, the head part and the body part? Notice how the head and the body elements are independent of each other. The HTML body falls outside of the head tag. Also, as you can clearly see from the example, the HTML body tag makes use of the <body> and </body> tags.

Novice HTML programmers usually make the mistake of putting the body element immediately below the title element in the head. This would be perfectly understand if you were writing a normal article. However, a body below a title element inside a head tag does not make an HTML body tag in HTML.

What you should do is open the body tag immediately after the closing head tag; as you can clearly see in our latest example. In between the body tags is where we would be nesting the contents of our website. In our previous example, we can clearly see that we have a paragraph element nested inside our body tag.

A paragraph element is just one of many elements that can be nested with an HTML body. Paragraph elements are characterized by the opening <p> and closing </p> tags. And if you still haven't figured it out, opening tags are created by enclosing the tag name between a lesser than symbol "<" and a greater than symbol ">". Closing tags, on the other hand, are pretty much written in the same way except for the forward slash symbol "/" that you have to put immediately after the lesser than symbol "<".

In our paragraph tag example, the opening paragraph tag is composed of the letter "p" enclosed between the greater than and the lesser than symbol "<>". When it comes to the paragraph closing tag, the letter "p" is preceded by a forward slash symbol "/" while both are still enclosed between the greater than and lesser than symbol.

HTML Paragraphs and Headings
Since we're talking about the paragraph element, know that the paragraph is the default element in HTML. This means that any content that does not have any distinguishable tag will automatically regarded by browsers as a paragraph. Therefore, if you don't want any particular content to be regarded by the browser as paragraphs, then you have to

apply some specific changes to them.

For example, you've written paragraph content and you want to give it a clear and distinguishable title. Surely you don't want to put it in between paragraph tags since it would just make it look like the rest of the paragraph. You can't move it outside of the paragraph tag since any content that doesn't have any distinguishable tag would automatically rendered as a paragraph by the browser.

In this case, what you want to do is nest and apply another modifying tag to the content that you wish to convert into a paragraph title. Note that the title that we're talking about here is not the HTML title within the head tag, but just a normal paragraph title in the body. We can do this with the help of the heading tag. Let's take a look at an example of this below:

```
1       <!DOCTYPE html>
2       <html>
3           <head>
4               <title>Learning HTML in 1 Day</title
5           </head>
6           <body>
7               <h1>How to Learn HTML in 1 Day or
Less</h1>
8               <p>Understanding HTML does have its
advantages</p>
9           </body>
10      </html>
```

Imagine how bland and monotonous it would be if all the contents of a website looked the same and had no structure whatsoever. Therefore, it is important to remember that when creating a nice and appealing website, always make sure that your content is structured properly. To do this, we must apply some headings.

Headings are tags that apply structure to website content. They do this by designating certain levels of importance to different parts of the content. In line seven of your previous example, You can see that we've applied a heading tag to the content "How to Learn HTML in 1 Day or Less"; specifically the heading 1 or <h1> tag..

Headings have six levels namely the h1, h2, h3, h4, h5, and h6. See an example of them below:

<h1> Heading 1 </h1>
<h2> Heading 2 </h2>
<h3> Heading 3 </h3>
<h4> Heading 4 </h4>
<h5> Heading 5 </h5>
<h6> Heading 6 </h6>

As you can see from the example above, the level of boldness and font size decreases from h1 to h6. The h1 heading, which has a large font size and high level of boldness, is applied to contents that have the highest level of importance. Examples of these are Titles, Chapter Headings, etc. The h2 heading, which possesses a level of boldness and font size that are two points lower than the h1 heading, is mainly applied to content that have a secondary level of importance. Examples of these are subtitles, sub-headings, sub-points, etc.

Use of the rest of the headings as you see fit so long as you're able to create structurally sound content. Let's see another example of how headings are applied below:

```
1       <!DOCTYPE html>
2       <html>
3               <head>
```

```
4               <title>How to Survive During A
Disaster</title>
5          </head>
6          <body>
7               <h1>Things to Take Care of During A
Disaster</h1>
8                    <h2>Securing Your Home</h2>
9                         <p>Secure          your
perimeter</p>
10                        <p>Secure  your  entry
points</p>
11                        <p>Know how to defend
from intruders</p>
12                   <h2>Procuring Supplies</h2>
13                        <p>Stock     up     on
Water</p>
14                        <p>Stock     up     on
Food</p>
15                        <p>Have    appropriate
clothing for every conditions</p>
16          </body>
17     </html>
```

To understand our example more clearly, it would be best if we can see how this HTML document would be rendered by the browser. To see how this is rendered, all you need do is save the file in HTML format (that's with a .html file extension) and open the file with the browser. It's that simple.

Here's how our HTML file would be rendered in the browser without using headings:

Things to Take Care of During A Disaster

Securing Your Home

Secure your perimeter

Secure your entry points

Know how to defend from intruders

Procuring Supplies

Stock up on Water

Stock up on Food

Have appropriate clothing for every conditions

Here's how our HTML file would be rendered when headings are applied in the content. In this case we used the heading 1 and the heading 2:

Things to Take Care of During A Disaster

Securing Your Home

Secure your perimeter

Secure your entry points

Know how to defend from intruders

Procuring Supplies

Stock up on Water

Stock up on Food

Have appropriate clothing for every conditions

Notice how our content appears bland and monotonous without the headings. There's no way to distinguish where the points of interest are in the content. After applying the headings however, you can clearly see from our second illustration that the main points of interest are clearly distinguished, there's a clear level of importance in the content, and it now has structure.

People who are new to HTML programming sometimes use headings the wrong way. For instance, they use headings to denote emphasis to a particular phrase or word in a content.

15

They even go as far as use headings whenever they just want to increase the font size or boldness of a particular paragraph, sentence, or phrase in a content. Know that this is not how headings should be used and is considered bad coding practice.

Headings should only be used to apply structure in a content and not as a means to increase font sizes and boldness. Here's another reason why you should only use headings as originally intended: Search Engine Optimization or SEO. If you're not familiar with SEO, think of it as the Internet standard for ranking websites in search engine search results. It presents certain rules and guidelines on how to make sure your website gets sufficient traffic by ranking high in search engine results.

In web development circles, people would always be sharing search engine optimization tips for their websites. One particular tip that you'll most likely hear often is to limit the number of heading 1's that you have on a web page. Some would even go as far as tell you that there's a rule stating exactly that; when in fact there isn't.

As a matter of fact, Google—the main authority when it comes to search engines and SEO—says that you won't get penalized for making use of multiple h1 tags, or any kind of heading tag for that matter, on a web page. However, they are keeping a close watch on whether you're using multiple headings of the same kind logically. If you're not using multiple headings of the same kind in a webpage logically, you'll get penalized by having a low search result ranking, which will have a drastic effect on your website traffic.

Another thing to remember about headings is that you have to utilize them in order. If you used an h1 prior, you can't immediately follow that with an h3 or an h6. You have to make use of them in order. You're not allowed to skip. It is also a good idea to plan your website in advance and think of the kinds of content you want to put on your website. This way, you'll be able to develop a heading strategy that will indicate the level of importance of the various sections of your website, based on those content.

Based on what we've discussed so far about headings, let's have one last example below:

```
1       <!DOCTYPE html>
2       <html>
3            <head>
4                 <title>Things to Consider When Buying
A Bike</title>
5            </head>
6            <body>
7                 <h1>Bike Type</h1>
8                    <h2>Road Bike</h2>
9                         <p>Trek</p>
10                        <p>Cannondale</p>
11                        <p>Cervelo</p>
12                    <h2>Mountain Bike</h2>
13                        <p>Santa Cruz</p>
14                        <p>Commencal</p>
15                        <p>Niner</p>
16                    <h2>Track Bike</h2>
17                        <p>Japanese      Keirin
bikes</p>
18                        <p>Look bikes</p>
19                        <p>Pinarello</p>
20               <h1>Frame Size</h1>
21                    <h2>Road Bike</h2>
22                        <h3>Men</h3>
23                             <p>4'10" - 5'0" =
47cm – 48cm frame size</p>
24                             <p>5'0" - 5'3" =
49cm – 50cm frame size</p>
```

```
25                              <p>5'3" - 5'6" =
51cm - 53cm frame size</p>
26                              <h3>Women</h3>
27                              <p>4'10" - 5'1" =
44cm - 46cm frame size</p>
28                              <p>5'1" - 5'3" =
47cm - 49cm frame size</p>
29                              <p>5'3" - 5'5" =
50cm - 52cm frame size</p>
30              </body>
31      </html>
```

Here's how it would be rendered in the browser:

Attributes

So what are HTML attributes? Generally, HTML attributes provide additional information about an HTML element. It is always declared within an element's opening tag and always comes in name-and-value pairs. For example, if we want to give our <html> tag a language attribute, then we can do it like this:

18

```
1       <!DOCTYPE html>
2       <html lang="en-US">
3             <head>
4                   <title>Learning How to Put Attributes
in HTML</title>
5             </head>
6       </html>
```

As you can see from the code above, we've incorporated a language attribute in our opening <html> tag. It should always come in a name-and-value format. In this case, "lang" is the name of the attribute, followed the equal sign which denotes designation, and then the value of the attribute which is "en-US". We're basically declaring that our example HTML document will have an English language format.

Putting a language attribute in the opening <html> tag isn't necessarily required for every HTML document. However, accessibility applications like search engines and screen readers need this piece of information in order to index your web page or website successfully.

Aside from the language attribute that we just discussed, there are still many other attributes that we can make use of in HTML. In order to keep this book as concise as possible, we won't be discussing all of them in-depth since there are so many of them that it would require a book on its own. However, we will go ahead and discuss some of the more common attributes used in HTML. Here they are in no specific order:

Anchor/Href attribute
The <a> tag or the anchor tag is the tag that you use every time you want to attach a URL to a word or group of words; converting it into a Hyperlink. The <a> tag is used in conjunction with the href attribute to specify the specific URL that will be attached to the text. Look at an example of this below:

```
1      <!DOCTYPE html>
2      <html>
3           <head>
4                  <title>Converting        Text        into
Hyperlinks</title>
5           </head>
6           <body>
7                  <p>If you want to go to Google.com, <a
href="http://www.google.com">click here</a></p>
8           </body>
9      </html>
```

Looking at line 7 of our code example, you can clearly see that we've enclosed the phrase "click here" within the attribute tag. We then used the href attribute to specify the URL that will be attached to the text. This process of converting normal text into a clickable link is called Hyperlinking. Hyperlinking is very useful in a sense that it makes your website and content look clean and efficient. In addition, creating a hyperlink instead of typing the whole URL saves significant space in your website.

Every time you feel the need to redirect/refer a website visitor to another affiliate or non-affiliate website, just create a hyperlink using the anchor tag and href attribute. If you're wondering how our example anchor tag and href attribute example would be rendered in a browser, look at the illustration below:

file:///home/root/Desktop/example1.html

If you want to go to Google.com, click here

As you may have probably noticed by now, a hyperlink is characterized by a clickable, blue-colored, underlined text. However, do note that hyperlinks exhibit color changes whenever their status change. For instance, if the hyperlink has been visited by the user during that particular session, it'll show a purple color. If the link is currently being viewed, it will therefore be deemed as active and will display a red color.

Image/Src attributes

One of the things that we can do to make websites more nice and appealing is put images in them. Almost all websites nowadays contain images. Images are what attracts visitors of all sorts to a website. Putting images in a website involves making use of the <img> tag and the src attribute. Let's go ahead and take a look at how this is done below:

```
1       <!DOCTYPE html>
2       <html>
3              <head>
4                     <title>Let's  put  a  picture  in  our
Website</title>
5              </head>
6              <body>
7                     <p>Take a look at the image below</p>
8                     <img
src="http://blogs.plos.org/obesitypanacea/files/2014/10/s
andwich.jpg" />
9              </body>
10      </html>
```

In line 8 of our example code, you can clearly see how we've used the <img> tag, the src attribute, and its image URL value to put an image on our HTML document. Let's take a look at how our code will be rendered in the browser:

Take a look at the image below

As you may have already noticed in our example, the <img> tag does not make use of a standard closing tag to be closed. We close the image tag by simply adding a space and a forward slash symbol "/" right after the value for the attribute. This is what you call a void element.

In addition to being able to indicate the source of the image using the src attribute, we can also indicate the image's dimensions; specifically its width and height. This is done by immediately adding the width and height attributes, both with their respective values, right after the src attribute and its value. Take a look at an example of this below:

```
1       <!DOCTYPE html>
2       <html>
3            <head>
4                    <title>Let's put a picture in our Website
and Resize it</title>
5            </head>
6            <body>
7                    <p>Take a look at the image below</p>
8                    <img          src="http://animalia-
life.com/image.php?pic=/data_images/raccoon/raccoon3.jp
```

```
g" width="120" height="80" />
9              </body>
10    </html>
```

Scaling attributes such as the height and width are usually applied to pictures/images that need scaling down in order to either save website real estate or fit the format of the website you're creating.

Image links

Clickable images that redirect you to another page or an entirely different website are fairly common these days. Using images as hyperlinks instead of normal text makes a website look more interesting, thus creating more appeal. In order to create an image link, all we need to do is nest an image element inside an anchor element. Let's look at how this is done in the code example below:

```
1      <!DOCTYPE html>
2      <html>
3            <head>
4                   <title>        Creating         Image
Hyperlinks</title>
5            </head>
6            <body>
7                   <a
href="http://www.google.com"><img
src="http://2.bp.blogspot.com/-NJTDTa6UZf4/U3Bu-
B5XrbI/AAAAAAAAOf8/yVCeh-yMr-k/s1600/google-logo-
874x288.png" /></a>
8            </body>
9      </html>
```

You can clearly see in line 7 of your code how we nested the two elements to form an image link. The logic behind why nesting these two elements creates an image link is simple. Remember that HTML is a mark-up language; all about marking content to know its type and give it some unique attributes. Since we want to make a hyperlink out of an image, HTML logic dictates that you have to mark that image up with something; specifically an anchor tag with the href attribute.

That's exactly what we did in our example. First we wrote the code for putting images in HTML, which is <img src="insert image URL here" />, and then we enclose that within the anchor tag to make it into a clickable hyperlink.

<a href="insert destination URL here"><img src="insert image URL here" /></a>

Image links doesn't showcase any immediately observable traits that may indicate that they are hyperlinks; apart from your mouse pointer turning into a hand once it is put over the image link.

CHAPTER 2:
HTML FUNDAMENTALS 2

Aside from what we've learned so far, there might come a time when you'll need to create listed content in y our website. Whether you're enumerating steps or making a shopping list, the use of lists in HTML is necessary. Lists in HTML come in two variants: Unordered and Ordered lists.

Unordered List

We make use of unordered lists in HTML every time we need to enumerate things in no specific order. For example, if we want to make a list of things to buy in a grocery store, we'll make use of the unordered list since the items enumerate can be bought in no specific order. Let's take a look how unordered lists are implemented in HTML code:

```
1     <!DOCTYPE html>
2     <html>
3          <head>
4                <title>Things    to    Buy    in    the
Grocery</title>
5          </head>
6          <body>
7                <h1>Food</h1>
8                <ul>
9                     <li>Eggs</li>
10                    <li>Bread</li>
11                    <li>Fruits</li>
12                    <li>Vegetables</li>
13               </ul>
14          <body>
15     </html>
```

As you can see from your example code—specifically lines 8 through 13—our unordered list element makes use of the <ul> and </ul> tags to indicate that the items that will follow are listed in no specific order. Of course, a list can only be a list if there are enumerated items. Therefore, to specify that a particular item content is a part of list, it should be enclosed between opening <li> and closing </li> list tags.

Unordered lists are usually rendered by the browser in bullet form. An unordered list's bullet style may vary depending on the value that's set for its type attribute. Here's an example of an unordered list's type attribute implemented in HTML code:

```
1     <!DOCTYPE html>
2     <html>
3         <head>
4             <title>Changing an Unordered List's Bullet Style</title>
5         </head>
6         <body>
7             <h1>Unordered List 1</h1>
8             <ul style="square">
9                 <li>item 1</li>
10                <li>item 2</li>
11                <li>item 3</li>
12            </ul>
13            <h1>Unordered List 2</h1>
14            <ul style="disc">
15                <li>item 1</li>
16                <li>item 2</li>
17                <li>item 3</li>
18            </ul>
19        </body>
20    </html>
```

Here in our example, we've made two unordered list with two different bullet styles; both using the style attribute. Remember to apply the list attribute on the opening list tag only. Do not, under any circumstances, apply it on the opening list tags of the items. Doing so would definitely yield an HTML error during rendering in the browser.

Here's what our code above would look like when rendered in the browser:

Unordered List 1

- item 1
- item 2
- item 3

Unordered List 2

- item 1
- item 2
- item 3

There another attribute that we can apply to our list, and that is the compact attribute. The compact attributes main purpose is to make the formatting of the list more compressed. Most HTML programmers use this attribute if there's limited space on the specific page where the list will go. Let's take a look at how this is implemented in HTML code:

```
1      <!DOCTYPE html>
2      <html>
3            <head>
4                  <title>How to Use the Compact
Attribute in a List</title>
5            </head>
6            <body>
7                  <h1>Compact List</h1>
8                  <ul compact="compact">
9                        <li>item 1</li>
```

```
10                          <li>item 2</li>
11                          <li>item 3</li>
12                  </ul>
13          </body>
14    </html>
```

And this is how it would be rendered by the browser:

Compact List

- item 1
- item 2
- item 3

As you can see from our illustration, the list is much more compressed than normal. Use the compact attribute on your list to make it fit on a web page with limited space. Also, notice how the name of the attribute and its value are the same; compact.

Ordered List

We make use of ordered lists in HTML every time we need to enumerate things in a particular order. Let's say we want to teach somebody how to bake a cake. To be able to successfully bake a cake, the steps on how to do it should be listed and followed in the correct order. Therefore, we make use of the ordered list. Here's an example of an ordered list in HTML:

```
1     <!DOCTYPE html>
2     <html>
3          <head>
4              <title>How to Bake a Cake</title>
5          </head>
6          <body>
7              <h1>Baking a Chocolate Cake</h1>
8              <ol>
9                  <li>step 1</li>
```

```
10                          <li>step 2</li>
11                          <li>step 3</li>
12                  </ol>
13              </body>
14      </html>
```

As you can see in our code, we use the <ol> tag to start our ordered list. And just like in our unordered list previously, we enclose the steps that we want to enumerate in our list between the opening <li> and closing </li> tags. Ordered lists make use of numberings instead of bullets. Let's see how our previous code example is rendered in the browser:

Baking a Chocolate Cake

1. step 1
2. step 2
3. step 3

As you can see from our illustration, the steps are numbered in the order that they should be followed. Similar to the unordered list, ordered lists have attributes of their own. They are:

- *Compact* – Again, similar to the unordered list compact attribute, this ordered list compact attribute renders the list in a much smaller fashion than normal. This attribute is perfect for when you need to insert an ordered list on a webpage that has limited real estate.
- *Reversed* – This ordered list attribute will organize the list in descending order. Be default, ordered lists are arranged in an ascending manner. However, if the need arises for the list to be arranged in a descending order, this is the attribute that you must use. This is perfect if you're doing a countdown of listed items for example.

- ***Start*** – The start attribute specifies at which point the ordered should start. If for any reason you need to start your list from a specific point other than the very beginning, this is the attribute that you should use. For example, you want to start your numbered list from the number 5, then all you need to do is put a "5" value for the start attribute; start="5".
- ***Type*** – Similar to our unordered list, the type attribute changes the ordered bullet style to a value other than the default numerical style. There are five common values for the type attribute that can be implemented in an ordered list. These are the default numerical style represented by the number "1", a capitalized alphabetical style represented by the letter "A", a non-capitalized alphabetical style represented by the small letter "a", a roman numeral style represented by the roman numeral "I", and a small letter "i" style, which is obviously represented by the small letter "i". The syntax for declaring the type of ordered list is similar to the unordered list as well, where style="value".

Nested lists

Just like how we can nest a tag within a tag, we can also nest lists within a list. Let's take a look at how this is done in HTML code:

```
1   <!DOCTYPE html>
2   <html>
3           <head>
4                   <title>Nested lists</title>
5           </head>
6           <body>
7                   <ol>
8                           <li>My Cars
9                                   <ul>
10                                          <li>Ferrari
Enzo</li>
```

```
11                          <li>Porsche
911</li>
12                              </ul>
13                          </li>
14                      <li>My Motorcycles
15                          <ul>
16                              <li>Honda
CBR</li>
17                              <li>Kawasaki
Ninja</li>
18                              </ul>
19                          </li>
20              </ol>
21              <ul>
22                  <li>"Favorite Pets"
23                      <ol>
24
    <li>Dog</li>
25
<li>Cat</li>
26
    <li>Chameleon</li>
27                          </ol>
28                      </li>
29                  <li>"Favorite Drinks"
30                      <ol>
31
    <li>Soda</li>
32                              <li>Iced
Tea</li>
33                          <li>Coffee</li>
34                          </ol>
35                      </li>
36              </ul>
37          </body>
38 </html>
```

38 lines of code can be a little bit daunting for first timers who are reading this book. So to gain a better understanding of nesting lists in HTML, let's see how our code is rendered in a browser:

1. My Cars
    ○ Ferrari Enzo
    ○ Porsche 911
2. My Motorcycles
    ○ Honda CBR
    ○ Kawasaki Ninja

- "Favorite Pets"
    1. Dog
    2. Cat
    3. Chameleon
- "Favorite Drinks"
    1. Soda
    2. Iced Tea
    3. Coffee

As you may have noticed already, nesting lists are no different than nesting any other element in HTML. All you need to do is declare the parent element first, and then put any other element you want to nest inside that parent element; and so forth.

In our example, we start our ordered list in line 7 with the <ol> tag. The first item in our ordered list is "My Cars", and the second item is "My Motorcycles".

Next, we inserted an unordered list under the first item (My Cars) in our ordered list. We did that by enclosing our whole unordered list element in between the <li> and </li> tags of our first ordered list element. This is clearly evident in lines 8 through 13 in our example HTML code above.

The same nesting process was done with the unordered list

in our example. Lines 21 through 36 of our example code clearly exhibit how an ordered list is nested within the first and second items of your unordered list. Take notice of each of the nested tag's indentation from their parent tags. You can clearly see that indentation greatly improves code readability.

Making HTML Comments
Putting comments in HTML code is considered good coding practice in today's standards. Think of comments as post-its notes designed to remind you what a particular block of HTML code is all about. Comments aren't part of the main executable HTML code, therefore it is written in such a way that it would be ignored by the browser during rendering. To see how comments are incorporated in HTML code, see the example below:

```
1       <!DOCTYPE html>
2       <html>
3            <head>
4                  <title>Learning How To Put Comments in HTML</title>
5            </head>
6            <body>
7                  <!--This is an example of a comment-->
8                  <p> A comments is written just above this paragraph tag</p>
9                  <!--The next code makes an ordered list-->
10                 <ol>
11                      <li>Notice another comment above the ordered list tag</li>
12                      <li>I think that's all for making comments in HTML</li>
13                 </ol>
14           </body>
15      </html>
```

Looking at our example above, line 7 and line 9 showcases comments made in an HTML code. Saving this HTML code in an .html file and opening it in your browser would reveal that during rendering, the comments are completely ignore by the browser and therefore wasn't displayed in the output. As what we have previously mentioned, a comment's job is to remind HTML programmers what a particular block or line of code is all about.

Also know that comments are also a type of tag. In order for a line of text to be recognized as a comment and not a paragraph, it must be enclosed within the opening comment tag and the closing comment tag. The opening comment tag is written as <!-- and the closing comment tag is written as -->. Look at lines 7 and 9 of our example code to see an example of this.

Font Sizing

Now that we've finished learning how to put comments in our HTML code, let's now proceed to discuss modifying the font sizes of our content. As what we have previously discussed, the paragraph is the default content format in HTML. Each time a line or block of text falls outside of any tag, it is automatically given a paragraph format. As a good coding practice, however, we make sure that whenever we want to give any content a paragraph format, we put them in between an opening and closing paragraph tag; <p> and </p>.

Similar to HTML lists, we can also designate certain attributes to paragraph tags. One of these attributes is the style attribute. The style attribute allows you to change numerous aspects on the paragraph. These aspects include but are not limited to font size, font color, font family, text alignment, background color, etc.

Let's go in-depth with the aforementioned aspects since

these are essential and is commonly used when creating a website. First, let's discuss how to change the font size using the style attribute. See the example HTML code below:

```
1      <!DOCTYPE html>
2      <html>
3           <head>
4                <title>First font size change</title>
5           </head>
6           <body>
7                <p style="font-size: 10px"> This is a tiny text! </p>
8                <p style="font-size: 20px"> This is a normal sized text!</p>
9                <p style="font-size: 40px"> This is a big text!</p>
10          </body>
11     </html>
```

Looking at our example above, you can see that we have three paragraphs nested inside our body tag. They all have style attributes and each has a value for changing the font size. Attributes are always inserted in the opening tag of an element, as you can clearly see in our example, and you saw this in our previous examples with href in <a> and src in <img>.

To change the font size of a paragraph, insert the "style" attribute in the opening <p> tag. Give your style attribute a value equal to "font-size", followed by a colon symbol ":", the size of the font that you want, and a "px" at the end. The "px" stands for the graphical unit of measurement called pixels. Lines 7 through 9 clearly show how to change the font size of a paragraph into different sizes.

Font Color

Now that we have learned how to change the font size, let's now discuss how to change the font color. In changing the font color, we're still going to use the style attribute. We then give the style attribute a value of "color", followed by a colon symbol ":", and then the color that you want the font to have. Let's take a look at an example of this below:

```
1      <!DOCTYPE html>
2      <html>
3          <head>
4              <title>Changing the font colors!</title>
5          </head>
6          <body>
7              <p style="color: green">This is a green
paragraph</h1>
8              <p style="color: violet">This is a violet
paragraph.</p>
9              <p style="color: red">This is a red
paragraph.</p>
10         </body>
11     </html>
```

As you can see in lines 7 through 8 of our code, different color values are assigned to the style attributes of each paragraph. One thing to take note of is that defining color names can be done in two ways. It can be defined using the name of the color itself, which is what we did in our example, or using a color's hexadecimal equivalent. For example:

```
1      <!DOCTYPE html>
2      <html>
3          <head>
4              <title>Changing the font colors!</title>
5          </head>
6          <body>
7              <p style="color: #00008B">This is a
dark blue paragraph</h1>
```

```
8                    <p style="color: #FF00FF">This is a
magenta paragraph.</p>
9                    <p style="color: #FFFF00">This is a
yellow paragraph.</p>
10           </body>
11     </html>
```

Notice how hexadecimal values are used to define color in our example above instead of color names. A color's hexadecimal value is used whenever a web designer wants use a combination of hue as font color.

Font Family

So far we've already discussed how to change the font size and font color in HTML. Next, let's see how to change the font type of our content in HTML. To change the font type, give your style attribute a value of "font-family", followed by a colon symbol ":", and then followed by name of the font. Let's look at how this is implemented in our example below:

```
1       <!DOCTYPE html>
2       <html>
3            <head>
4                  <title>Changing Font Styles</title>
5            </head>
6            <body>
7                  <h1>Examples of font styles</h1>
9                  <p style="font-family: Arial">This is
Arial.</p>
10                 <p style="font-family: Verdana">This is
Verdana.</p>
11                 <p style="font-family: Impact">This is
Impact.</p>
13           </body>
14     </html>
```

Look at lines 9 through 10 in our example HTML code above.

37

Notice how changing the font style is almost similar to how you change the font color or font size. First you insert the style attribute in the opening tag of the element that you want to apply the changes to, followed by the font-family declaration and then the name of the font that you want the element font to change into.

One great thing about the style attribute is that its usage is not only limited to paragraphs. You can use the style attribute with other elements such as headings and lists as well. Also, all of the style values that we have discussed so far can be used simultaneously in one element. Let's take a look at an example of this below:

```
1   <!DOCTYPE html>
2   <html>
3       <head>
4               <title>Loving the font changes</title>
5       </head>
6       <body>
7               <h1 style="font-family: Arial">Big title</h1>
8               <ol>
9                       <li style="font-family: Arial; font-size:
16px; color: red">This item is big Arial.</li>
10                      <li style="font-family: Verdana; font-
size: 12px; color: blue">This item is medium Verdana.</li>
11                      <li style="font-family: Impact; font-size:
10px; color: green">This item is small Impact.</li>
12              </ol>
13      </body>
14  </html>
```

Just like what we mentioned previously, you can also use the style attribute on other elements aside from the paragraph. In lines 7, 9, 10 and 11 of our example code, you can clearly see that we've incorporated the style attribute with the heading <h1> element and the items in the ordered list element. Not only that, we've also defined three values, namely font-family, font-size and color, under each instance of the style attribute simultaneously.

This is what makes the style attribute awesome. It allows us to change numerous aspects of the font all in one sweep.

Background Color
In the previous section, we've already covered techniques on how to change the different aspects of a font. Now, let's discuss how to change to background color of a particular HTML element. To change the background color of an element, we'll be making use of the style attribute once more. Let's look at an example code below on how to change an element's background color:

```
1      <!DOCTYPE html>
2      <html>
3            <head>
4                  <title>Extremely    nice    background
color!</title>
5            </head>
6            <body style="background-color: brown">
7                  <h3>Favorite Racing Bikes</h3>
8                        <ol      style="background-color:
yellow">
9                              <li>The             Trek
Madone</li>
10                             <li>The  Pinarello  Dogma
F8</li>
11                             <li>The Cervelo S5</li>
12                        </ol>
13           </body>
14     </html>
```

Look at lines 6 and 8 in our example above. As you can see, there's a close resemblance between changing a font's size/type/color and changing the background color of an element. To change the background color of an element, insert the style attribute in the opening tag of the element that you want to change. After that, give the style attribute a value of "background-color", followed by a colon symbol ":", and then the name of the color. Similar to changing the font color, you can also replace the color name with its hexadecimal equivalent.

Aligning Text in HTML
Next well discuss how to align text in HTML. Aligning text in HTML is crucial for a professional looking website. Text alignment is also extremely important whenever we want to put a structure in our content. Generally, it would be nice to be able to move the text around so as to create space to insert another element on the webpage.

Text alignment comes in three types: Center, Left and Right. Again, when aligning text, we're going to make use of the style attribute. To align text, simply insert the style attribute inside the opening tag of the text that you want to align, follow it up with a "text-align" value, put a colon symbol immediately after "text-align", and then the location of the alignment that you want last. See an example of this below:

```
1       <!DOCTYPE html>
2       <html>
3           <head>
4               <title>How to Align Text!</title>
5           </head>
6           <body>
7               <h3 style="text-align: center">Favorite
Movies</h3>
8                   <ol>
9                       <li      style="text-align:
left">Star Wars</li>
10                      <li      style="text-align:
center">Top Gun</li>
```

```
11                              <li        style="text-align:
right">The Ring</li>
12                          </ol>
13              </body>
14      </html>
```

Text alignment is pretty straightforward. Just use the style attribute with a define text alignment value and you're good to go. You'll be able to align text from any of the three locations; left, right or center.

Bold Text

There are many reasons why an HTML programmer would want to make a text in bold. A word may need to be depicted with strong emphasis or maybe there's a need for the word to stand out from the rest. Converting a line or a block of text into bold is just a matter of enclosing the text in between the opening and closing strong tags. Let's take a look at an example of this below:

```
1       <!DOCTYPE html>
2       <html>
3           <head>
4                   <title>How  to  make  write  text  in
bold!</title>
5           </head>
6           <body>
7                   <p>Are      you       trying      to
<strong>sing</strong>?</p>
8                   <p>No      I     am      not.      I'm
<strong>too</strong> busy eating candy.</p>
9           </body>
10      </html>
```

Converting normal text into bold is child's play, as you can see in our example. Just enclose the word or group of words in between the <strong> and </strong> tags and you'll be able to turn them into bold text.

Emphasis

Aside from converting text into bold, there are times when we want to italicize words to show emphasis. Similar to converting text into bold, we can italicize words by enclosing the text we want to emphasize in between the opening and closing emphasis tags. Let's take a look at an example of this below:

```
1      <!DOCTYPE html>
2      <html>
3          <head>
4              <title>How to Italicize Words</title>
5          </head>
6          <body>
7              <p>Is he a <em>genius</em>?</p>
8              <p>No   he   is   not.   He's   just
<em>educated</em>.</p>
9          </body>
10     </html>
```

As you can see in lines 7 and 8 of our code, we've enclosed the word genius and educated in between the <em> and </em> tags. When viewed from a browser, the words "genius" and "educated" will be italicized. You may also nest the emphasis <em> tag within the strong <strong> tag if you want to text to stand out with emphasis. Just make sure to close both both tags in the order that they are opened.

So there you have it. In this chapter we've learned about indentation, creating ordered and unordered lists, making comments in HTML code, changing the font's size, shape and type, changing the background color of an element, aligning text and putting emphasis on text using bold and italicization. We've sure come a long way.

In the next chapter we'll discuss how to create tables in HTML.

CHAPTER 3:
HTML FUNDAMENTALS 3

Our HTML learning has been progressing nicely so far. If you're reading this chapter, it means that you now know more about HTML than when you started reading chapter one. We've already discussed how to create a basic HTML file, how to create paragraphs, headings, links and images, how to change the font's size, type and color, and lastly, how to create text emphasis via bolding and italicizing.

In this chapter, we'll discuss some of the important structural aspects of HTML, specifically the <table>, <span>, and <div>. First let's discuss the tables or <table>.

Tables
Tables are very important in presenting data in HTML. There may be instances where data needs to be displayed in tabular form on a website or webpage. This is where tables come in handy. Tables not only make reading tabular data easy, but also present information in a neatly fashion using columns and rows.

Tables are basically just a bunch of data arranged in columns and rows. Tables are defined with the table <table> tag. To create the other aspects of a table in HTML, you'll be enclosing them within the opening <table> tag and the closing </table> tag. One such aspect would be the table row.

To create a table row, the <tr> must be used. Let's look at the example below on how to define the table and its rows in HTML code:

```
1      <!DOCTYPE html>
2      <html>
```

```
3              <head>
4                   <title>Creating Tables in HTML</title>
5              </head>
6              <body>
7                   <table>
8                        <tr></tr>
9                        <tr></tr>
10                  </table>
11             </body>
12        </html>
```

As you can see in our example code above, we've created a table by nesting a <table> and </table> tag within the body tag. In between the <table> and </table> tags, we've nested two lines of <tr> and </tr> tags which depicts the table's rows. An important thing to remember about tables in HTML is that we never really create table columns per se. Instead, you just specify the number of cells each row must have and that automatically create columns for your table.

Cells, or table data, are created with the use of the <td> tag. A table data <td> basically act as containers for different elements like text, lists, and images, just to name a few. If you run the aforementioned HTML code example, you'll see that the browser doesn't render any tables at all. Do not worry. The reason why nothing is rendered is because we haven't specified a border for our table yet. The table's rows are already rendered; we just can't see them yet since there are no borders to distinguish it from the rest of the background.

Let's go ahead and create a table with rows and cells or table data in HTML below:

```
1        <!DOCTYPE html>
2        <html>
3              <head>
4                   <title>Creating Tables in HTML</html>
```

```
5          </head>
6          <body>
7               <table>
8                    <tr>
9                         <td>Data 1</td>
10                   </tr>
11                   <tr>
12                        <td>Data 2</td>
13                   </tr>
14                   <tr>
15                        <td>Data 3</td>
16                   </tr>
17              </table>
18         </body>
19    </html>
```

As you can see in the example above, we've created a table with three rows. Each of those rows has a cell or table data. Looking at this come from a browser, you'll see that the data are just arranged on top of one another. It doesn't look like a table at all since there are no borders.

To put a border on our table, we must make use of the border attribute. Just like any attribute, we must insert it at the opening tag of the element where you want the attribute to be applied. Let's take a look at our previous example below, but this time with borders incorporated into it:

```
1     <!DOCTYPE html>
2     <html>
3          <head>
4               <title>Creating Tables in HTML</html>
5          </head>
6          <body>
7               <table border="1px">
8                    <tr>
9                         <td>Data 1</td>
```

```
10                              </tr>
11                              <tr>
12                                      <td>Data 2</td>
13                              </tr>
14                              <tr>
15                                      <td>Data 3</td>
16                              </tr>
17                      </table>
18              </body>
19      </html>
```

Looking at line 7 of our example HTML code above, you can see that we've applied the border attribute to your table element. Similar to the way we change the font size of a text, we assign a pixel value to our border attribute to determine the table's border thickness; in this case we assigned a value of 1 pixel, which is the thinnest.

It may not seem much, but you just learned how to create a single column table in HTML. Now let's go ahead and create another column for our table. As what was mentioned prior, there's no way to create additional table columns in HTML. Instead, we horizontally add cells in a row to give the illusion of creating a column. Let's see how this is done in the example code below:

```
1       <!DOCTYPE html>
2       <html>
3               <head>
4                       <title>Adding Columns in HTML</title>
5               </head>
6               <body>
7                       <table border="1px">
8                               <tr>
9                                       <td>Ball</td>
10                                      <td>Red</td>
11                              </tr>
```

```
12                          <tr>
13                              <td>Umbrella</td>
14                              <td>Blue</td>
15                          </tr>
16                      </table>
17                  </body>
18      </html>
```

Remember that rows always go on a horizontal manner. Logically, if you add a new cell in a row, it could only go one way; horizontal. Therefore, if you keep on adding cells in each row, you're virtually creating a column. Let's try and render the above code in the browser.

The illustration above shows how our previous HTML code example is rendered in the browser. Notice how two new columns are formed after adding a second cell for each row in our table. Each time a cell is added in a row, they sit beside each other forming the illusion of a second column.

Table Heads
The tables we have made so far in our previous examples don't look much. They're look bland and lack structure. To

make our tables look the part, we'll make use of table heads and bodies. In an HTML document, the head tag contains information on what the webpage is all about, while the body tag contains all the contents of the website or webpage.

In the same way, the table head contains information about the table and the table body houses the actual tabular data or information. Since we dealt with tabular data in our previous examples, let's go ahead and put them in between opening and closing table body tags. Then, let's go ahead and create a table head tag for our table. Look at the example below:

```
1       <!DOCTYPE html>
2       <html>
3              <head>
4                      <title>Tables in HTML</title>
5              </head>
6              <body>
7                      <table border="1px"">
8                      <thead>
9                              <tr>
10                                     <th>Bike
Type</th>
11                                     <th>Price</th>
12                              </tr>
13                      </thead>
14                      <tbody>
15                              <tr>
16                                     <td>Trek
Madone</td>
17                                     <td>MSRP
$3,400</td>
18                              </tr>
19                              <tr>
20                                     <td>Pinarello
Dogma F8</td>
21                                     <td>MSRP
$4,499</td>
```

```
22                          <tr>
23                        </tbody>
                  </table>
24          </body>
25    </html>
```

As you can see from in our code, our table now has a heading. This gives it a more refined and professional look. Notice we've nested both the <thead> tag and the <tbody> tag within in the <table> tag.

In order to put a cell where the table data for our heading will be placed, we must first claim a row for it. You can clearly see that we've put a row for our heading in lines 9 and 12 of our sample code. Now that our heading has its own designated row, we can now put cells or table data within them. We do this be nesting table heading tags <th> within the table rows of our table head:

```
8                    <thead>
9                      <tr>
10                        <th>Bike
Type</th>
11                        <th>Price</th>
12                      </tr>
13                   </thead>
```

Notice that unlike when we're handling tabular data, we're now using the <th> tag as a place holder for the headings of our table columns instead of <td>. Remember that just like any other tag, it is imperative that you don't forget to close them. Look below for the browser rendered version of our previous HTML code example:

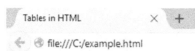

file:///C:/example.html

Bike Type	Price
Trek Madone	MSRP $3,400
Pinarello Dogma F8	MSRP $4,499

Naming Tables in HTML

Now that we've learned how to put column headings in tables, it's now time to move forward and learn how to name tables in HTML. Just like most titles, whether it is a title on an essay or a title on a webpage, we want it to go all across the top of the content; in this case, our table. To achieve that, we will be using an attribute called "colspan". Think of colspan as merging the cells into one just like in Microsoft Excel.

Let's take a look at an example of how colspan is incorporate in HTML:

```
1      <!DOCTYPE html>
2      <html>
3          <head>
4              <title>Tables in HTML</title>
5          </head>
6          <body>
7              <table border="1px"">
8                  <thead>
9                      <tr>
10                         <th colspan="3">Bike Chart</th>
11                     </tr>
12                     <tr>
13                         <th>Bike Type</th>
```

```
14                              <th>Price</th>
15
        <th>Availability</ht>
16                                  </tr>
17                              </thead>
18                              <tbody>
19                                  <tr>
20                                      <td>Trek
Madone</td>
21                                      <td>MSRP
$3,400</td>
22                                      <td>Yes</td>
23                                  </tr>
24                                  <tr>
25                                      <td>Pinarello
Dogma F8</td>
26                                      <td>MSRP
$4,499</td>
27                                      <td>out          of
stock</td>
28                                  <tr>
29                              </tbody>
30                          </table>
31              </body>
32      </html>
```

If you look at lines 9 through 10 of our code, you can see that in order to put a name to your table that spans the whole top row using colspan, you must first create the entire row where the table name will go (clearly seen in line 9 where we opened a <tr> tag). Once you've created the row, all you need to do is create a table header using the <th> tag and apply a colspan attribute that has a value of the number of columns that you want it to go across; in this case, 3 columns. Below is an example of how the previous code would be rendered in the browser:

Bike Chart		
Bike Type	**Price**	**Availability**
Trek Madone	MSRP $3,400	Yes
Pinarello Dogma F8	MSRP $4,499	out of stock

Table Styles

Now that we know how to make a complete border in HTML, the next thing that we'll do is put some style in our table to make it look more appealing. Check the code below out and then we'll go through the attributes that makes a table stylish line by line:

```
1       <!DOCTYPE html>
2       <html>
3         <head>
4           <title>Table Time</title>
5         </head>
6
7         <body>
8
9           <table style="border-collapse:collapse;">
10            <thead>
11              <tr>
12                <th colspan="2" style="color: red">Famous
Monsters by Birth Year</th>
13              </tr>
14              <tr style="border-bottom:1px solid black;">
15                <th   style="padding:5px;"><em>Famous
Monster</em></th>
16                <th   style="padding:5px;border-left:1px
solid black;"><em>Birth Year</em></th>
```

```
17              </tr>
18            </thead>
19            <tbody>
20              <tr>
21                <td style="padding:5px;">King Kong</td>
22                <td     style="padding:5px;border-left:1px
solid black;">1933</td>
23              </tr>
24
25              <tr>
26                <td style="padding:5px;">Dracula</td>
27                <td     style="padding:5px;border-left:1px
solid black;">1897</td>
28              </tr>
29
30              <tr>
31                <td     style="padding:5px;">Bride     of
Frankenstein</td>
32                <td     style="padding:5px;border-left:1px
solid black;">1944</td>
33              </tr>
34            </tbody>
35          </table>
36
37        </body>
38      </html>
```

And here's how it looks like when rendered in a browser:

Famous Monsters by Birth Year

Famous Monster	*Birth Year*
King Kong	1933
Dracula	1897
Bride of Frankenstein	1944

Let's start dissecting our code from line 9. As you can see this time around, instead of just declaring our table's border to 1px using the border attribute, we've now declared an overall style for our table using the style attribute. For your style attribute, we've assigned it with a "border-collapse:collapse" attribute value.

So what does the border-collapse property do? What the border-collapse property basically does is it specifies whether the borders of our HTML table are collapsed into either separate mode (which is the default mode in HTML) or single border mode. The border-collapse has four different property values namely:

Collapse – With this property value, the borders of the table will be collapsed into a single border whenever possible. This means that border-spacing and void-cell properties will be bypassed.

Separate – With this property value, the borders of the table will be detached. This means that border-spacing and void-cell properties will be disregarded. This is basically the default border style in HTML.

Inherit – When you give the border-collapse property with the Inherit value, you're basically giving this element the same value as its parent element. Of course, this is under the assumption that you've nested a table within another element. If the table element that you're assigning this property value is not nested, then this would definitely not work.

Initial – Initial and Separate are basically the same. It sets the property back to its original value.

Let's take a look at the illustration below and see how elements with these property values are rendered in the browser:

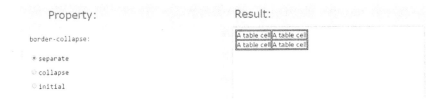

As you can see from your illustration above, we have the border-collapse property value set to separate. You'll notice that with the Separate value, the cells are separated by individual borders making it look like there are four small boxes (the cells) inside one big box (the table border).

Result:

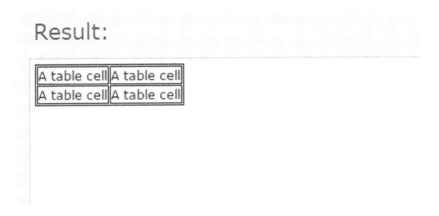

Now let's see how the table would look like if it has a property value of collapse:

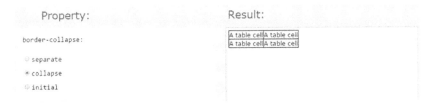

As you can clearly see from your example above, the cells aren't separated with each other. The collapse property value removes the inner borders on all the cells giving it the appearance that they are all collapsed together.

We will not be showing an example of the Initial property value here since it yields the same output as the Separate property value. Now let's move forward with the rest of our HTML analysis.

In line 12 of our last code example, we made use of this line of code:

```
<th colspan="2" style="color: red">Famous Monsters by Birth Year</th>
```

What we're doing in this line of code is we're basically setting the parameters of our Table name. We're making use of the colspan attribute and giving it a value of 2 to make your Table name span two columns. We also gave it a style attribute with a color property that has a value of "red". This means we're giving your Table name a red font color.

In lines 14 through 17 of our code we're basically setting the parameters of our table head names.

```
14   <tr style="border-bottom:1px solid black;">
15                  <th    style="padding:5px;"><em>Famous Monster</em></th>
16                  <th    style="padding:5px;border-left:1px solid black;"><em>Birth Year</em></th>
17   </tr>
```

Keep in mind that our table has no overall border defined. The divisions for the individual cells are there, but it is not clearly apparent because there's no general border attribute applied to our <table> tag; which is okay since we want to make the table have a similar style to the one below:

56

Famous Monsters by Birth Year

Famous Monster	Birth Year
King Kong	1933
Dracula	1897
Bride of Frankenstein	1944

In line 14, you can clearly see that we've put applied a style attribute to the 2nd row of our table which is part of the table head. We're basically giving the 2nd row of our table head a bottom border of 1 pixel that's solid black:

<tr style="border-bottom:1px solid black;">

This gives both cells where our table headers "Famous Monster" and "Birth Year" are contained, have a solid black border at the bottom.

In line 15, we're giving our table header "Famous Monster" a style attribute that has a padding property value of 5 pixels. So what is padding? Padding is one of three things that comprise an HTML box model. An HTML box model basically works something like this:

Say for example you have a cell. A cell of course is composed of the content that has a border around it. The area inside the border where the content/data is placed is called the element box. Know that the content/data within contained within then border doesn't necessarily touch the border itself. It is surrounded by a space called the padding box.

Think of the padding box as a margin between the content and the border. Now the area in which the border is placed is called the border box. The border box is basically as think or as thin as the border itself. Around the border is a space that basically prevents other elements from being too close. It is called the Margin box.

So basically when you say padding, we're talking about the space around the element inside the border. So when you set a padding value for a particular attribute, you're basically setting how much space there would be between the content/data and the border itself. We can clearly see this implemented in lines 15, 16, 21, 22, 26, 27, 31, and 32 of our code.

When there's no padding value set, the data or content may be oriented at any point within the cell. By setting a padding value, we're basically centering the content inside the cell since padding goes around it entirely. You'll also notice that we've enclosed our table headers "Famous Monster" and "Birth Year" inside emphasis tags; <em> and </em>.

Emphasis tags basically have a visual function and an audio function. On the visual side, it denotes emphasis by italicizing text. On the audio side, it denotes emphasis by stressing the enunciation of the word. This is only evident when the HTML code is read by a screen reader for the visually impaired.

With that being said, understanding the rest of our code example for applying Styles in tables comes easy. It's just a matter of putting together certain attributes and properties to get the desired effect.

Division Tags

Compartmentalization is a crucial whenever you're working on a large scale HTML project. Coding one large chunk of code makes coding more tedious and confusing. Therefore, dividing your website into sizable chunks may become necessary. By dividing your website into workable portions, you're able to work on certain elements much faster and significantly make debugging code easy, since you don't have to go and look over thousands of lines of code.

In order to divide our web pages into more workable containers, we have to make use of the division tag <div>. Let's take a look at the code below to see how the division tag is used:

```
1      <!DOCTYPE html>
2      <html>
3           <head>
4                <title>Result</title>
5           </head>
6           <body>
7                <div  style="width:50px;   height:50px;
background-color:red"></div>
8                <div  style="width:50px;   height:50px;
background-color:blue"></div>
9                <div  style="width:50px;   height:50px;
background-color:green"></div>
10             <div    style="width:80px;    height:100px;
background-color:yellow"></div>
11           </body>
12     </html>
```

Just like when we define rows in an HTML table, the individual rows are not visible unless you specify a border.

The same thing applies when using the division tags. In our example code, we've specified the exact width and height of the division and applied a background color to it to make it visible.

Making use of divisions smartly will ultimately help you to create various HTML objects such as menus, sidebars, etc. In addition, you can also make the divisions you create clickable, just like how you make images clickable. How? By enclosing them within anchor tags of course. Here's an example of this below:

```
1       <!DOCTYPE html>
2       <html>
3               <head>
4                       <title>Result</title>
5               </head>
6               <body>
7                       <div style="width:50px; height:50px;
background-color:red"></div>
8                       <div style="width:50px; height:50px;
background-color:blue"></div>
9                       <div style="width:50px; height:50px;
background-color:green"></div>
10                      <a href="http:www.google.com"><div
style="width:50px; height:50px; background-
color:yellow"></div></a>
11              </body>
12      </html>
```

See how we enclosed our division within the anchor tag that has an href attribute in line 10? Creating new things out of something is fairly straightforward by using nesting in HTML. Let's see how the code above is rendered in a browser:

Now we can't show you how the last yellow division is clickable. However, if you can type the same code in your HTML editor, save it as an HTML file, and open it with a browser, you'll see that when you put your mouse pointer over the last yellow division, it'll turn into a hand icon; indication that it's a clickable hyperlink.

Span Tags

While division tags let you slice your web page into smaller chunks that you can individually style, Span gives you control over the styling of several smaller parts of your web page, such as text. For instance, if you require the first two words of your paragraph content to have a red font, you can enclose those two words within <span> and </span> tags and give them a red font color using CSS.

Let's take a look at an example of this below:

```
1      <!DOCTYPE html>
2      <html>
3           <head>
4                <title>The Gutsy Ninja</title>
5           </head>
6           <body>
7                <p><span      style="color:red">Gutsy
Ninja</span> wears a baseball cap and carries a samurai
sword.</p>
```

```
8          </body>
9       </html>
```

In our example, you'll see that we've enclosed the first two words of our paragraph inside the span tag with a style attribute that has a property value of "color:red". Normally, the style attribute would apply its color value to the entire paragraph. However, since we applied the style attribute to the opening span tag that encloses only the first two words, the style would only be applied to that content.

These tags are kind of tricky sometimes so let us go ahead and see one more example:

```
1       <!DOCTYPE html>
2       <html>
3           <head>
4               <title>Result</title>
5           </head>
6           <body>
7               <p>My favorite snacks are <span
style="font-family:Impact">Oreos and Chips</span>!</p>
8           </body>
9       </html>
```

Yes, you guessed it right. Colors aren't the only attribute that you can specifically change with the span tags. As you can see from our example above, you can even change the font type used in your content. In line 7, you'll notice that we gave our style attribute a value of font-family: Impact. This is will change the type of font for the content that is enclosed inside the span tag.

There are many other style attributes that you can apply to text based content. The font color and font size are just some examples of style attributes that you can apply in your content.

Have you ever wondered how those clickable pictures in your Facebook page are made? Using everything that we've learned so far, let's create a nice clickable picture album using HTML. This time around we'll also show what CSS does and how it is incorporated in HTML code.

We'll go step-by-step in the coding process to ultimate create a simple picture album online. We'll create a simple 3x3 photo album for now. Let's start with the code below:

```
1       <!DOCTYPE html>
2       <html>
3               <head>
4                       <link type="text/css" rel="stylesheet" href="stylesheet.css" />
5                       <title>My Online Photo Album</title>
6               </head>
7               <body>
8                <table>
9                 <tbody>
10                <tr>
11                  <td></td>
12                  <td></td>
13                  <td></td>
14                </tr>
15                <tr>
16                  <td></td>
17                  <td></td>
18                  <td></td>
19                </tr>
20                <tr>
21                  <td></td>
22                  <td></td>
23                  <td></td>
24                </tr>
25                 </tbody>
26                </table>
```

```
27            </body>
28      </html>
```

Defining the dimensions of your element is extremely crucial in HTML. There will be times when you'll be asked to work on a project website that has extremely limited space. Therefore, you have to be able to compress or constraint certain elements to fit it perfectly with the rest of the page. In the case of our online photo album here, we're initially defining its dimensions by specifying the number of rows and columns that it will have.

As you can see in lines 8 through 24 of our code, we've made three rows (line 10, 15, and 20) and within those 3 rows we've made three cells for each. As what we've mentioned before, making successive cells in a horizontal fashion basically gives the illusion that we're creating columns in an HTML table.

Notice that we haven't defined any style attribute for our table yet. The reason for this is because the cells in our table would only act as containers for the images that we will be putting in our online photo album. Putting our images in side these cell containers would allow us to better control the images' alignment to each other, their dimensions, and their proximity to each other.

You might also be wondering what the HTML code in line 4 mean. The tag that we're using in line 4 of our code is called a Link <link> tag. No, this is not another tag that creates hyperlinks. What the <link> tag does is basically create a linkage between an HTML document and another document that's located externally. It is typically used in linking external style sheets; specifically CSS.

The Link Element/Tag
You may also have noticed that the <link> element does enclose any kind of element. Instead, it contains only

attributes. Again, just like what we discussed before, elements like the one we used in line 4 is called a void element. This type of element should only be placed within the head of an HTML document. It could, however, appear multiple times within the HTML document as long as it is within the head.

We make use of the link tag every time we make use of CSS in our HTML document. The link tag has three attributes namely:

Rel – The rel attribute basically defines the relationship between the source document (HTML) and the document being link to, which is Stylesheet/CSS.

Type – The type attribute basically defines the type of media of the document being linked. Since we're linking a stylesheet/CSS document, the value would therefore be text/css.

Href – The href attribute basically defines the location of the document that's being linked. Usually, the href attribute would get a URL value. However in our case, just to be able to give out an example, we'll just give the stylesheet's filename as the href attributes value (stylesheet.css).

Now let's go ahead and move on to the next part of our code:

```
1       <!DOCTYPE html>
2       <html>
3              <head>
4                      <link type="text/css" rel="stylesheet"
href="stylesheet.css" />
5                      <title>My Online Photo Album</title>
6              </head>
7              <body>
8                <table>
```

```
9              <thead>
10                <th colspan="3">
11                    My Online Photo Album
12              </th>
13            </thead>
14            <tbody>
15            <tr>
16              <td></td>
17              <td></td>
18              <td></td>
19            </tr>
20            <tr>
21              <td></td>
22              <td></td>
23              <td></td>
24            </tr>
25            <tr>
26              <td></td>
27              <td></td>
28              <td></td>
29            </tr>
30            </tbody>
31            </table>
32          </body>
33      </html>
```

Similar to what we did in our previous HTML table examples, we gave our table a head so anybody who's looking at our photo album would know what it's all about. As you can see in lines 9 through 13 of our code, we've declared a single-row table head that spans 3 columns with a text-based content saying "My Online Photo Album".

Incorporating CSS in HTML

This next part would be how to incorporate CSS in HTML. As you know, CSS is an external document that's being linked to HTML so it can apply various aesthetic attributes to elements in HTML. To be able to apply a stylesheet in HTML, we must first create the stylesheet document itself. We do this by creating a file in any normal text editor and save it with a .css file extension. In our example, we've already specified the name of our CSS document as stylesheet.css.

Think of CSS as a predefined element attribute value chart. A typical CSS document would look like this:

```
1       img {
2               width:150px;
3               height:150px;
4       }
5
6       table, td {
7               borders: 2px #70b8ff solid;
8       {
```

As you can see from our example CSS document above, the <img> element's attribute and value is defined by enclosing the values inside curly brackets. In line 5 lies a whitespace; an empty space separating one element from the next. In line 6, the values of the next element's attributes are defined; also within curly brackets.

What our CSS document basically says is all <img> elements should have a width and a height attribute of 150 pixels, while tables <table> and its cells <td> should have a border that's 2 pixels in thickness, blue-colored, and should be a solid line. Remember how we noticed earlier that our table element has no style attribute whatsoever? This is because we need not put the attribute in HTML at all. We just have to define them in CSS so that every time we call that particular element, it would automatically have the attributes and values that are defined in the stylesheet.

Let's now go ahead and put some images on the HTML code

of our online photo album:

```
1       <!DOCTYPE html>
2       <html>
3              <head>
4                      <link  type="text/css"  rel="stylesheet"
href="stylesheet.css" />
5                      <title>My Online Photo Album</title>
6              </head>
7              <body>
8                <table>
9                  <thead>
10                     <th colspan="3">
11                             My Online Photo Album
12                     </th>
13                 </thead>
14                 <tbody>
15                 <tr>
16                     <td><img            src="http://globe-
views.com/dcim/dreams/ball/ball-05.jpg" /></td></td>
17                     <td><img            src="https://encrypted-
tbn2.gstatic.com/images?q=tbn:ANd9GcRsHqXNU44I9YlWN
H7I8brwLiUk3ILNeJxWlysCZ9oB3mPv2sGQ" /></td>
18                     <td><img            src="https://encrypted-
tbn0.gstatic.com/images?q=tbn:ANd9GcTuLELPmhlEGO0Xz
8x2k6baC64diYVmYcNl2qf7VzjeyUTqahE8DQ" /></td>
19                 </tr>
20                 <tr>
21                     <td><img            src="https://encrypted-
tbn1.gstatic.com/images?q=tbn:ANd9GcTsqE_k994Afwh_Fd
81pr6XPwFJj1cmxt14hfrRqJhU-7zq3SvcaA" /></td>
22                 <td><img
src="http://www.salsc.org/files/50.jpg" /></td>
23                 <td><img
src="http://www.toysrus.com/graphics/tru_prod_images/3
-Mini-Sports-Balls----pTRU1-6355189dt.jpg" /></td>
24                 </tr>
```

68

```
25                  <tr>
26                      <td><img        src="https://encrypted-
tbn2.gstatic.com/images?q=tbn:ANd9GcRkgFL5hoFq50LBiE
mnA5414t8dYaJneeSiILFBs7OzDc7cTvrsCg" /></td>
27                      <td><img        src="https://encrypted-
tbn1.gstatic.com/images?q=tbn:ANd9GcSTqAGgWXynsHjBO
SBZo3Cf3E6m7SOh4A-LAUiBMdmo_T6TbkFCCw" /></td>
28                      <td><img        src="https://encrypted-
tbn2.gstatic.com/images?q=tbn:ANd9GcQTa23jDZk3Xxgp3D
D8pbKleAr0Y7ZbTNtn9eqcQ3RDA0vxoM-Nvw" /></td>
29                  </tr>
30                  </tbody>
31              </table>
32          </body>
33      </html>
```

To better understand our photo album HTML code now that
we've placed images, let's go ahead and see how this is
rendered in the browser:

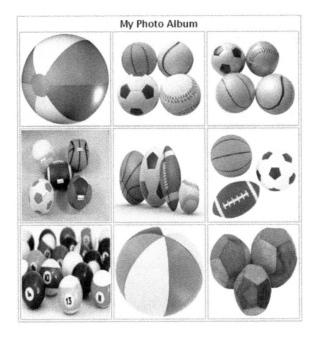

Again, we can see the power of nesting in HTML. To be able to place images within the cell containers of our table, we have to nest the images inside the table data/cell elements. That is exactly what we did in our example. If you take a look at all the image sources one-by-one, you'll find that the images are of different sizes. How did we manage to make them all have the same dimension? We did it with the use of CSS of course.

If you remember our last CSS document example, we've already defined the width and height attribute values for the <img> element. So every time we declare an <img> element in HTML, it'll automatically have the attributes and values defined in CSS. This is what makes styling content in HTML easy.

You'll also notice that our table <table> element and its individual cells <td> have a blue-colored, solid border that's 2 pixels in thickness. That's because we've also predefined the attribute values of our table and cell elements in CSS.

Of course any online photo album wouldn't be complete without clickable pictures. There are a lot of reasons for a web designer to want to make the pictures inside an online album clickable. Either they want to redirect the user to a page which houses the high resolution version of the picture being clicked, or they want to redirect the user to next picture in the album. Whatever the reason may be, making pictures clickable is the way to go.

We're going to make the pictures in our album clickable just like the way we converted an image into a hyperlink in the previous chapter; by enclosing the image element inside the anchor tag that has a href attribute.

Here's our photo album HTML code with clickable images:

```
1       <!DOCTYPE html>
2       <html>
3               <head>
4                       <link  type="text/css"  rel="stylesheet"
href="stylesheet.css" />
5                       <title>My Online Photo Album</title>
6               </head>
7               <body>
8                 <table>
9                   <thead>
10                      <th colspan="3">
11                              My Online Photo Album
12                      </th>
13                  </thead>
14                  <tbody>
15                  <tr>
16                      <td><a      href="www.google.com"><img
src="http://globe-views.com/dcim/dreams/ball/ball-
05.jpg" /></a></td>
17                      <td><a      href="www.yahoo.com"><img
src="https://encrypted-
tbn2.gstatic.com/images?q=tbn:ANd9GcRsHqXNU44I9YlWN
H7I8brwLiUk3ILNeJxWlysCZ9oB3mPv2sGQ" /></a></td>
18                      <td><a      href="www.xlibris.com"><img
src="https://encrypted-
tbn0.gstatic.com/images?q=tbn:ANd9GcTuLELPmhlEGO0Xz
8x2k6baC64diYVmYcNl2qf7VzjeyUTqahE8DQ" /></a></td>
19                  </tr>
20                  <tr>
21                      <td><a    href="www.youtube.com"><img
src="https://encrypted-
tbn1.gstatic.com/images?q=tbn:ANd9GcTsqE_k994Afwh_Fd
81pr6XPwFJj1cmxt14hfrRqJhU-7zq3SvcaA" /></a></td>
22                      <td><a  href="www.facebook.com"><img
src="http://www.salsc.org/files/50.jpg" /></a></td>
23                      <td><a      href="www.essays.ph"><img
src="http://www.toysrus.com/graphics/tru_prod_images/3
-Mini-Sports-Balls----pTRU1-6355189dt.jpg" /></a></td>
```

```
24                  </tr>
25                  <tr>
26                  <td><a        href="www.vimeo.com"><img
src="https://encrypted-
tbn2.gstatic.com/images?q=tbn:ANd9GcRkgFL5hoFq50LBiE
mnA5414t8dYaJneeSiILFBs7OzDc7cTvrsCg" /></a></td>
27                  <td><a        href="www.hotmail.com"><img
src="https://encrypted-
tbn1.gstatic.com/images?q=tbn:ANd9GcSTqAGgWXynsHjBO
SBZo3Cf3E6m7SOh4A-LAUiBMdmo_T6TbkFCCw"
/></a></td>
28                  <td><a        href="www.gmail.com"><img
src="https://encrypted-
tbn2.gstatic.com/images?q=tbn:ANd9GcQTa23jDZk3Xxgp3D
D8pbKleAr0Y7ZbTNtn9eqcQ3RDA0vxoM-Nvw"
/></a></td>
29                  </tr>
30                  </tbody>
31                </table>
32              </body>
33           </html>
```

If you look at lines 16 through 28 of our code, you'll see that we've enclosed the images within anchor tags that have URL href attributes. All-in-all, we've basically nested an image element, within an anchor element, within a cell element, within an HTML table element. If you render our photo album code in a browser, you'll notice that your mouse pointer now turns into a hand, which indicates that the images are now clickable.

This is fantastic. After what we've discussed from chapter 1 up to this point, you're now able to create a fantastic-looking online photo album. We've combined creating a table with rows and columns, put images inside the table's cells and make them clickable, and apply aesthetic attributes such as image dimensions, and border color and types to create our very own online photo album.

From this point onwards, feel free to try out new things such as increasing the number of images or create two separate albums within one page. You're only limited by your own imagination. HTML is also about experimenting and discovering new things.

CHAPTER 4:
CSS IN-DEPTH

CSS is a completely different topic on its own and is a very broad subject that warrants its own separate how-to guide. However, today's standard call for CSS's usage in almost every HTML website there is and therefore must be discussed to a certain extent in every HTML curriculum.

As what we've mention in previous chapters, CSS stands for Cascading Style Sheets. A stylesheet is basically a separate document that defines how an HTML should look like when rendered in a browser. The reason why it is called a cascading stylesheet is because the stylesheets can apply formatting to content when multiple styles already apply.

For example, let's say we want all our paragraph content to have a red font. We can actually pick out one paragraph specifically to have a yellow font. CSS can definitely do that. Let's take a look at our example HTML code below and its corresponding stylesheet:

```
1       <!DOCTYPE html>
2       <html>
3           <head>
4               <link type="text/css" rel="stylesheet" href="stylesheet.css"/>
5               <title>Fancy Fonts</title>
6           </head>
7           <body>
8               <p>The Ink that I used to write this sentence is blue. However, the ink I used to write the word "<span>pen</span>" is red!</p>
9           </body>
10      </html>
```

Its corresponding style sheet document is:

```
1      p {
2              color: blue;
3      }
4
5      span {
6              color: red;
7      }
```

If your render our example HTML code in the browser with this stylesheet, it'll have this output:

The Ink that I used to write this sentence is blue. However, the ink I used to write the word "pen" is red!

Similar to our photo album HTML code, we link our external stylesheet to this code via the link tag. Looking at our CSS document, we're defining attributes for two HTML elements; the paragraph <p> element and the <span> element. Our CSS document basically states that paragraphs will have a blue-colored font, while span elements will have red-colored fonts.

Looking at the rendered output, you can see that as soon as we used the elements listed in CS in our HTML code, the attribute values specified in CSS are immediately applied. Using CSS is just that easy.

What we're doing with CSS basically is separating the style formatting (CSS) from the structural content of an HTML document. Doing these has three main benefits:

- It gives you the ability to apply the exact same style to numerous elements in HTML without writing the code repeatedly. For instance, if you don't have CSS and you want to make all your paragraphs have the same font color, you have to put a style attribute inside all paragraph opening tags. If you have CSS, however, you just have to define the attribute for the paragraph element once in a CSS document.

- If you're working on multiple HTML documents and you want each of those documents to have the same style, you can just reference one single CSS file for every one of them. This makes coding and applying styles much faster and more efficient.

- Another benefit of separating style formatting from the main HTML code is you don't have to change each and every style tag whenever you want to implement big style changes to your content. All you have to do to make a site-wide style change is modify the CSS file and that's it.

There are actually two ways to put create CSS in one place. The first is by making use of the style tag inside the head of the HTML document. Inside the style tag you'll nest the various element attributes that you want to apply in the HTML document. Look at an example of this below:

```
1       <!DOCTYPE html>
2       <html>
3           <head>
4               <style>
5                   p {
6                       color: red;
7                   }
8               </style>
9               <title>The Red Ink</title>
10          </head>
11          <body>
12                  <p>Check out this paragraph written in
bright red ink!</p>
```

```
13          </body>
14     </html>
```

As you can see in lines 4 through 8 of our example HTML code above, we've created a style element where the CSS styles are nested.

The second way, which is considered by many as the best way, is by linking an external CSS document to the HTML document via the <link> tag. We've already made use of this when we made our online photo album in the last chapter. Let's take at look at another example of this below:

```
1      <!DOCTYPE html>
2      <html>
3           <head><link type="text/css"; rel="stylesheet";
href="stylesheet.css"/>
4                <title>The Paragraph with the Big Red
Font</title>
5           </head>
6           <body>
7                <p>The font size of this paragraph is 35
pixels and has a red font color.</p>
8           </body>
9      </html>
```

And here is its corresponding CSS/stylesheet document:

```
1      p {
2           font-sizes: 35px;
3           color: red;
4      }
```

Here's a point to remember whenever you use the link tag to link an external CSS document in HTML: 4Tthe values for the type and rel attributes of the link element are constant. Every time you make use of the link element, make sure that the type attribute always have the "text/css" value, and the rel attribute always have the "stylesheet" value. The only link attribute that may change is the href attribute since file locations for the CSS document may vary from project to project.

CSS Syntax
You may already have noticed that the CSS syntax is totally different from HTML. Most people who haven't used or even heard of CSS before have this false notion that CSS syntax is difficult to understand. They couldn't be more wrong. The CSS syntax is basically divided into three parts namely:

- Selector – The selector is basically the HTML element that you want to implement style changes to. Examples of these are <img>, <table>, <p>, and <td>, just to name a few.
- Property – The Property is basically the attribute of the HTML element that you want to implement style changes to. Examples of these are font, font-size, font-family, and color, just to name a few.
- Value – Lastly, Value is basically what it is. It is the attribute/Property's value. This is the one that specifies the specific style that needs to be applied on the HTML element. Examples of these are red (when it comes to color), Impact (when it comes to font-family), and 35 (when it comes to font-size).

The format of writing CSS syntax is as follows:

```
1    selector {
2    properties: value;
3    }
```

In the CSS syntax, you first must indicate the selector followed by an opening curly bracket. One the second line, define the property of the selector, follow it up with a colon symbol ":" and then the value. After the specifying the value, you must end the line with a semi-colon symbol ";". The semi-colon symbol tells CSS that you're done defining the property-value pair and you're ready to indicate the next. Lastly, since you opened up property-value pair with an opening curly bracket, you must also end it with a closing curly bracket on line three.

Another thing to keep in mind about CSS syntax is that you can also set multiple properties for a single selector. Here's an example:

```
1    p {
2        color: purple;
3        font-families: Trebuchet;
4        font-sizes: 32px;
5    }
```

As you can see in our example CSS document, we've defined three properties for the "p" selector. This is like hitting three birds with one stone. If we apply this CSS stylesheet to an HTML document such as this:

```
1    <!DOCTYPE html>
2    <html>
3        <head>
4            <link type="text/css" rel="stylesheet" href="stylesheet.css"/>
5            <title>Styling with CSS in HTML</title>
6        </head>
7        <body>
8            <p>Styling paragraph content in HTML with CSS is fun and easy!</p>
9        </body>
10   </html>
```

It would have this output when rendered in a browser:

CSS Comments

Just like HTML, writing comments in CSS is also crucial. Writing comments in code definitely helps in reminding you why you did something in a particular way. In addition, it will also help another HTML programmer to understand why implemented code in a certain way.

In CSS, comments are written in this format:

/*Put Your CSS Comments Here!*/

As you can see, CSS comments start with a forward slash symbol "/", followed by an asterisk "*", and then followed by the comment itself. After writing the comment, follow it up with another asterisk "*", and then lastly, another forward slash symbol "/".

Keep in mind that just like in HTML, browsers completely disregard comments when compiling HTML code for rendering. But just because they are being disregarded during rendering doesn't mean you shouldn't put them at all. Putting comments should be practiced at all times since it is considered good HTML coding practice.

So there you have it. You now have a firm grasp of HTML fundamentals. Keeping all the points we've discussed so far in mind will definitely help you in designing entry-level websites online. Thank you and we hope that we've taught you a lot about HTML in this book.

CONCLUSION

Now that you have a firm understanding of HTML's fundamentals, it is now up to you to explore and experiment with other attributes, techniques, and elements in HTML. Learning HTML is very easy as long as you keep the fundamentals that are indicated in this book in mind. Aside from HTML, also try to go in-depth with CSS. CSS is a great supplemental tool for HTML and would definitely help you create better, more dynamic websites.

Thank you for purchasing this book and we hope that we've helped you in learning HTML effectively.

CHECK OUT THE OTHER
ICODE ACADEMY BOOKS

1. HTML & CSS for Beginners: Your Step By Step Guide To Easily Learn HTML & CSS Programming In 7 Days

2. Java Programming: Your Step By Step Guide to Easily Learn Java in 7 Days

3. Python Programming: Your Step By Step Guide to Easily learn Python in 7 Days

www.ingramcontent.com/pod-product-compliance
Lightning Source LLC
La Vergne TN
LVHW052310060326
832902LV00021B/3806